This Book Belongs to

_____

Tony R. Smith

2020 S.S. PUBLISHING ALL RIGHTS RESERVED

Thank you for buying this book

SIGN LANGUAGE FOR KIDS

Tony R. Smith

Copyright © 2020 by Tony R. Smith. All Rights Reserved. No part of this publication may be reproduced, distributed, or transmitted in any form or by any means, including photocopying, recording, or other electronic or mechanical methods, or by any information storage and retrieval system without the prior written permission of S.S. Publishing, except in the case of very brief quotations embodied in critical reviews and certain other noncommercial uses permitted by copyright law

A

B

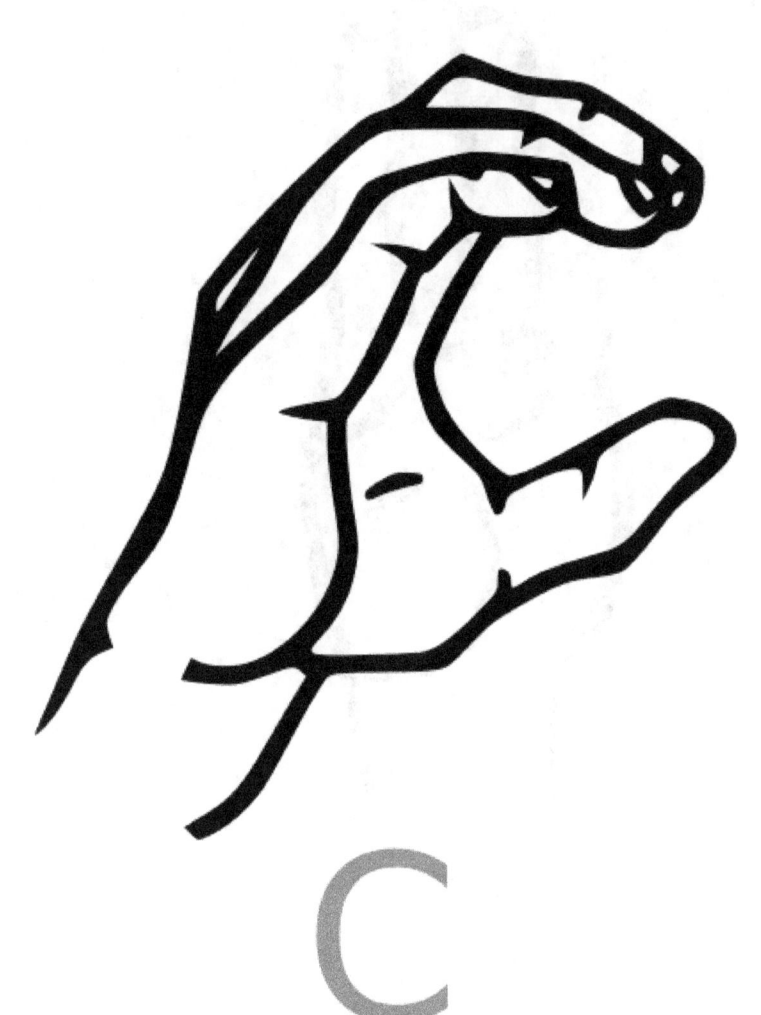

C

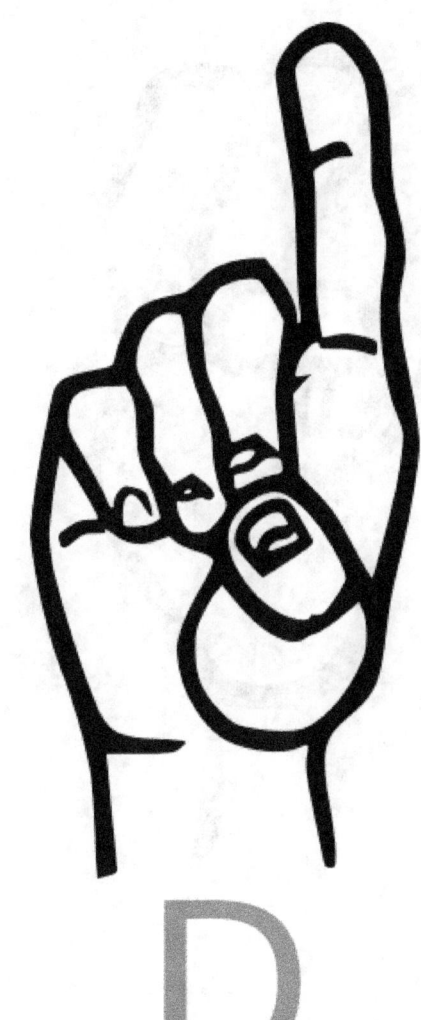

D

E

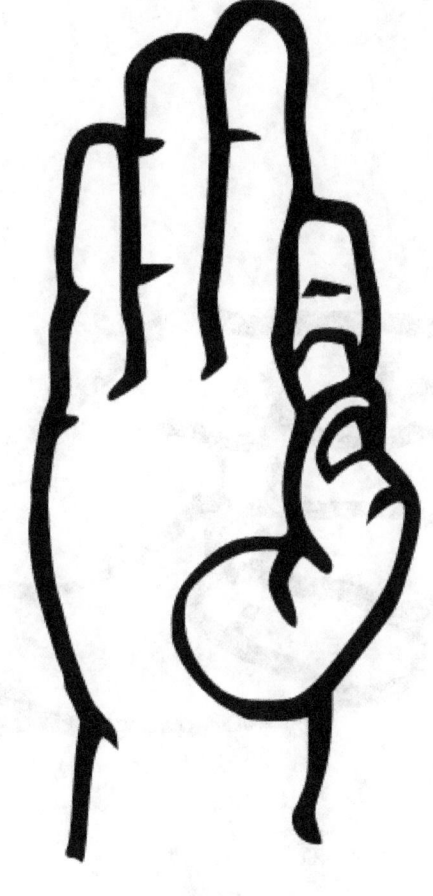

F

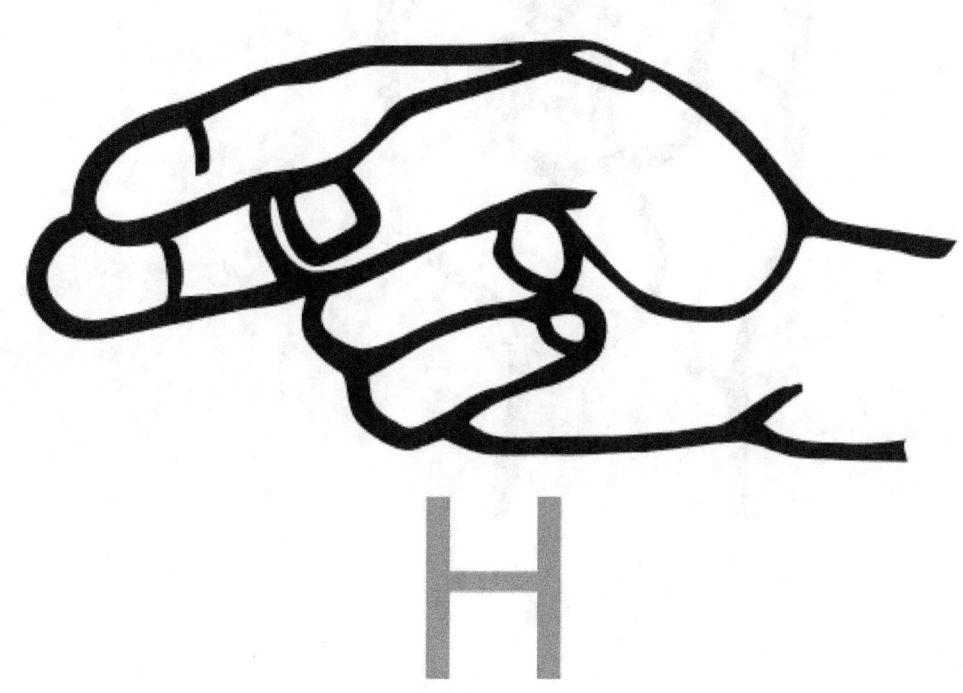

H

I

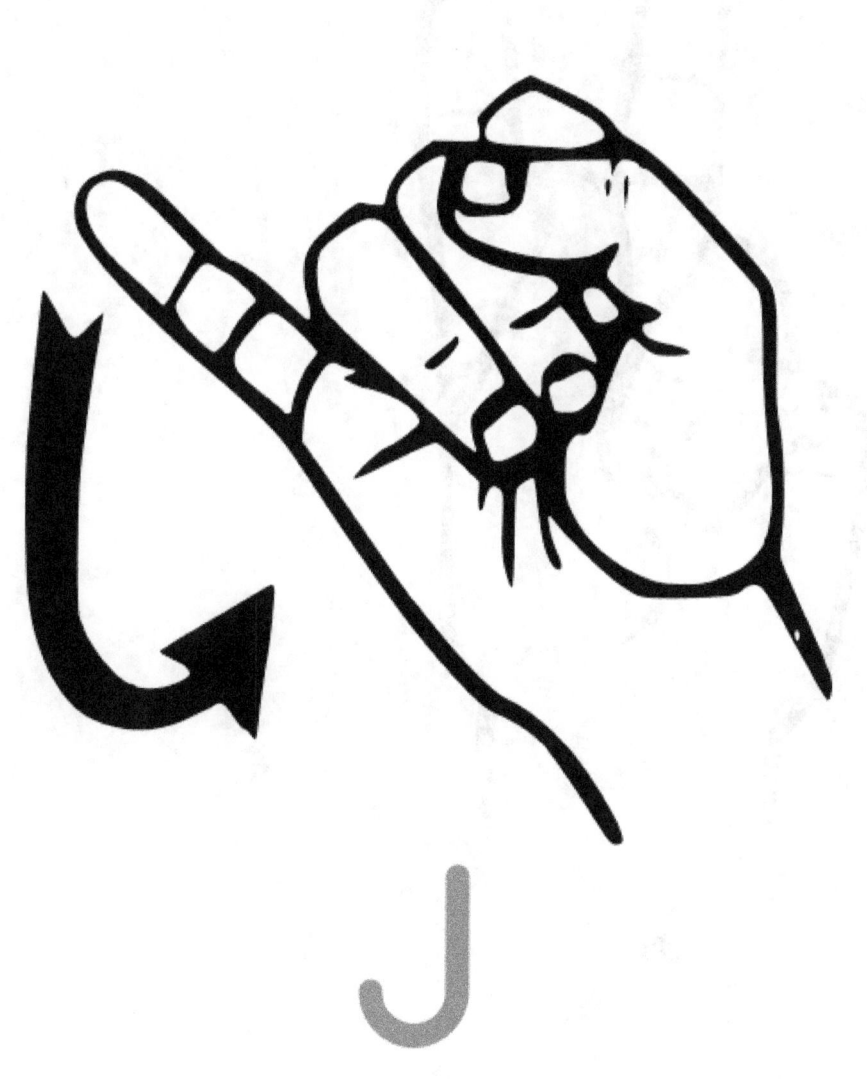

J

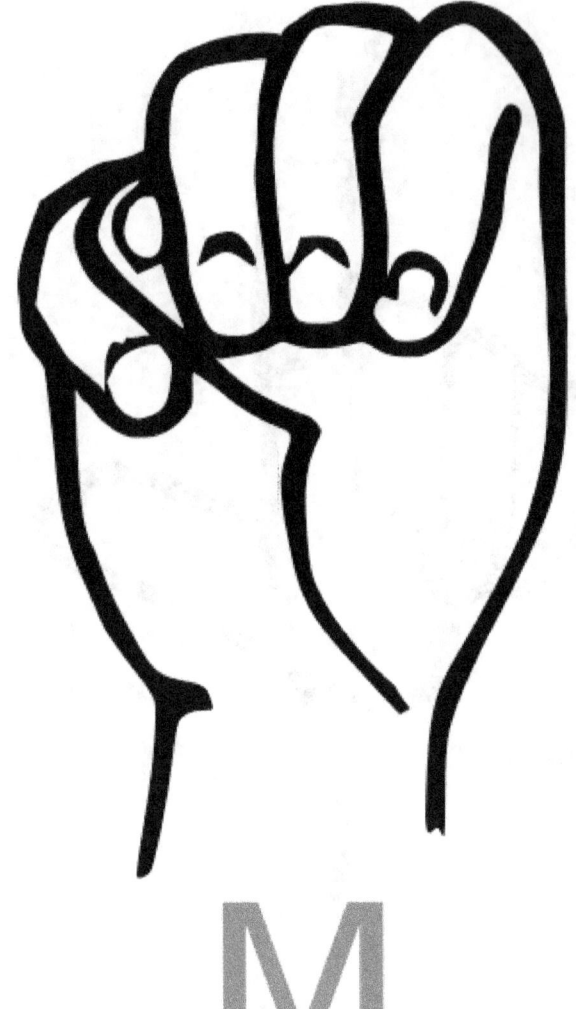

N

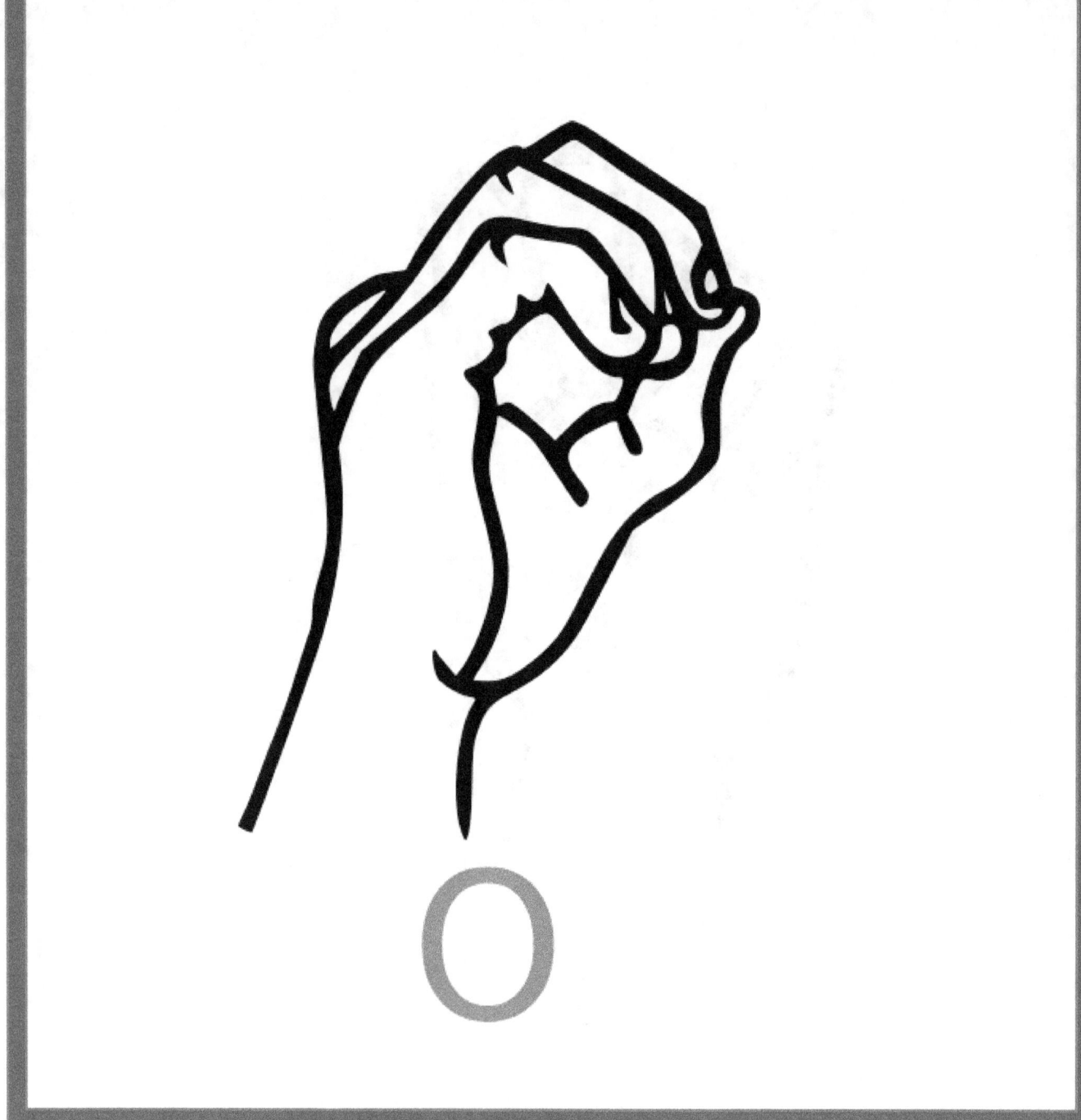

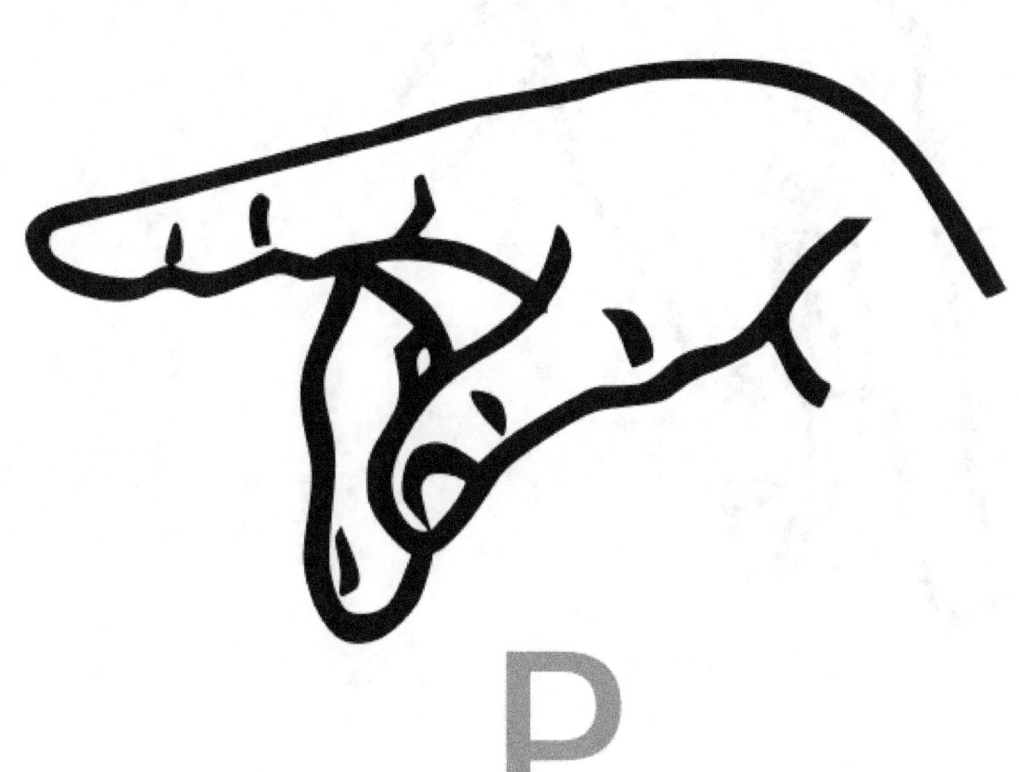

P

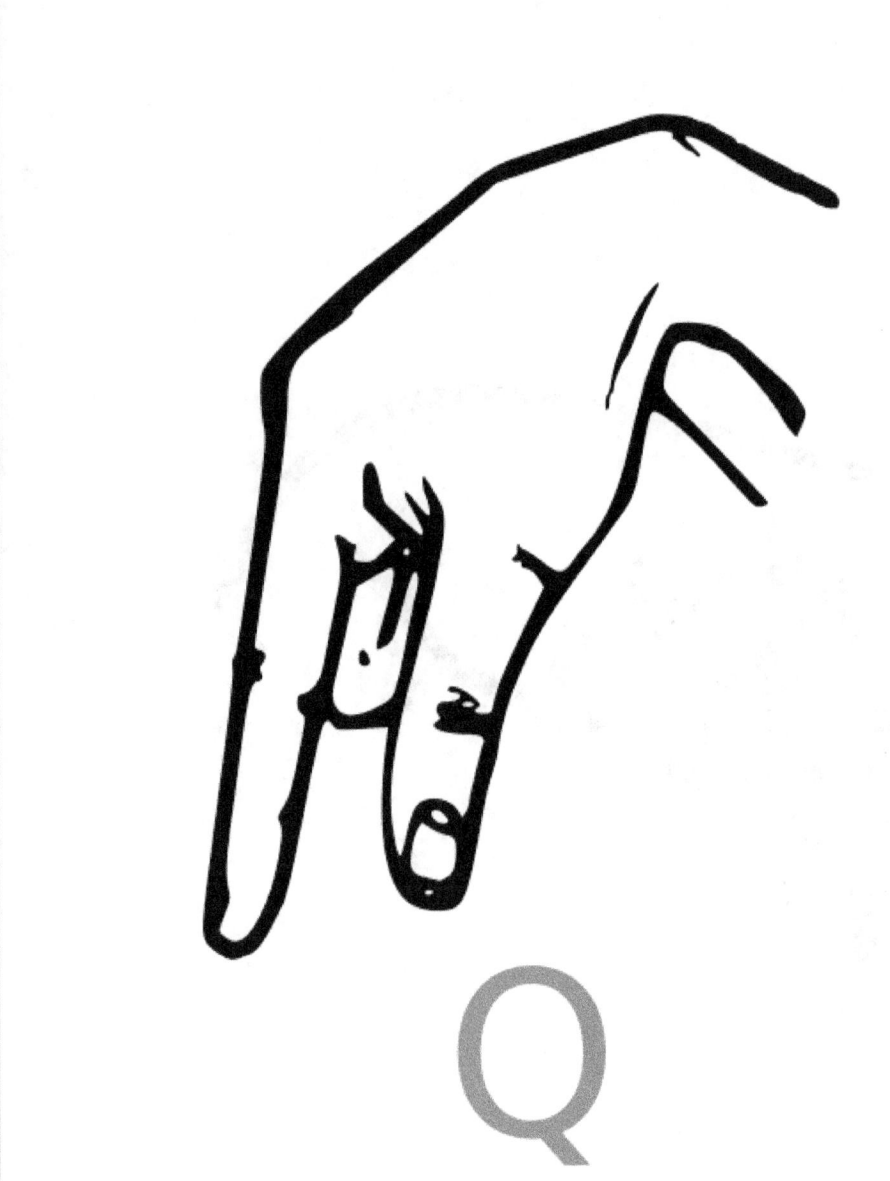

Q

R

S

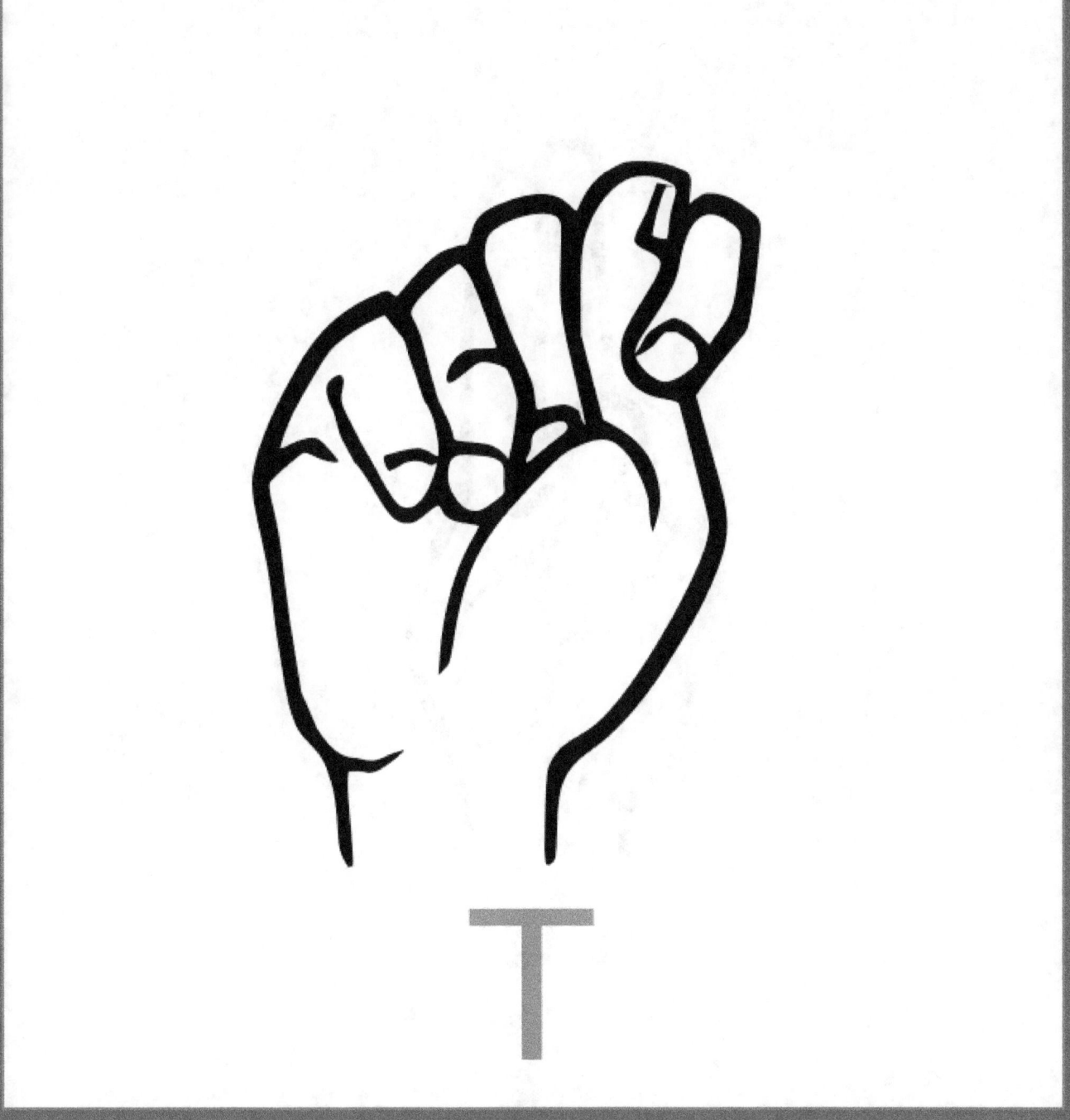

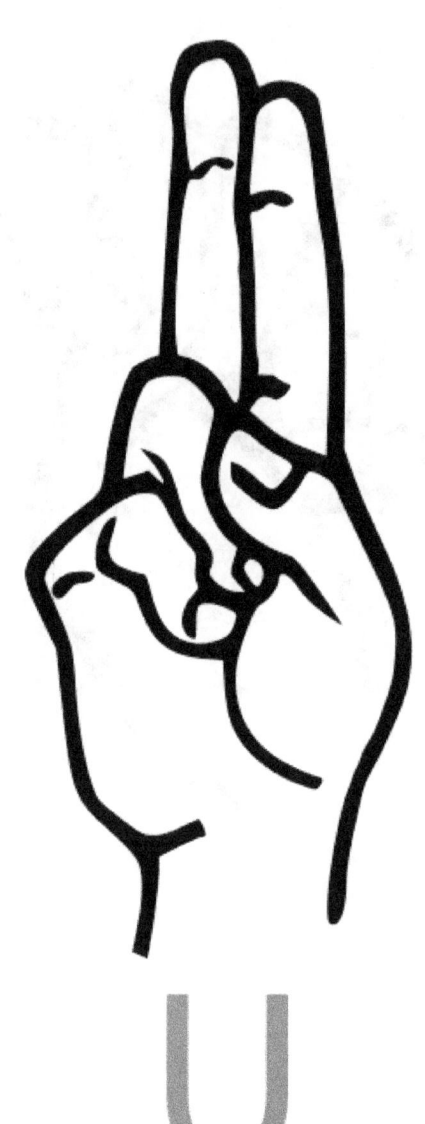

U

V

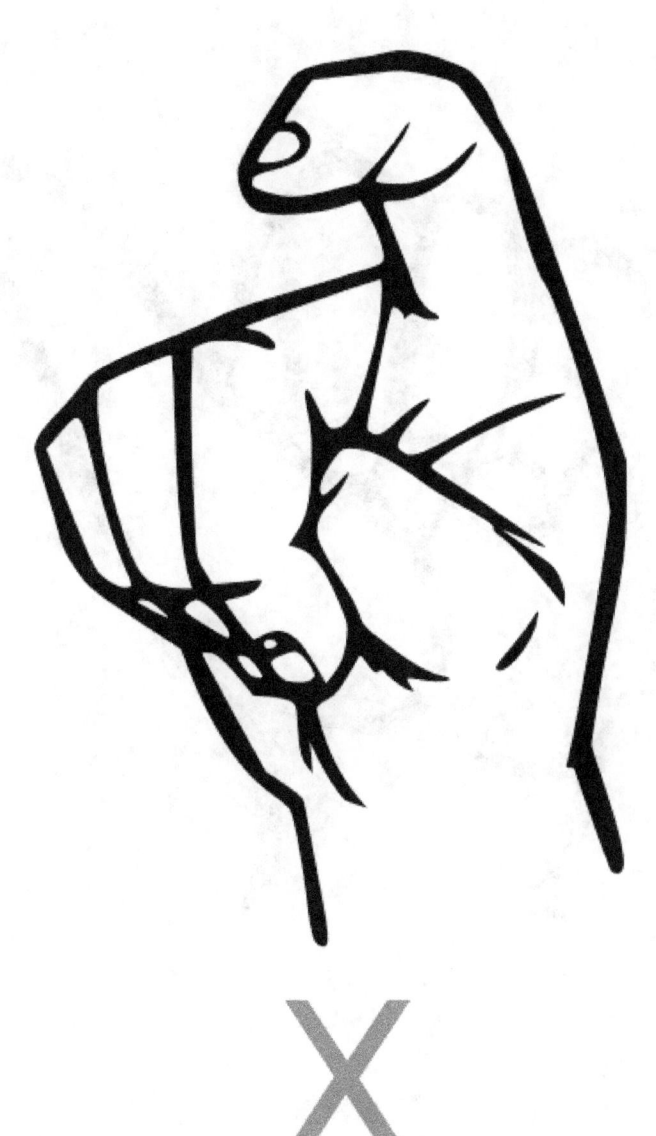

X

Numbers

Fill in the Number

5	3			7				
6			1	9	5			
	9	8					6	
8				6				3
4			8		3			1
7				2				6
	6					2	8	
			4	1	9			5
				8			7	9

ZERO

0

ONE

1

TWO

2

THREE

3

FOUR

4

FIVE

5

SIX

6

SEVEN

7

EIGHT

8

NINE

9

TEN

10

Emergency Room Talk

Admit/Enter 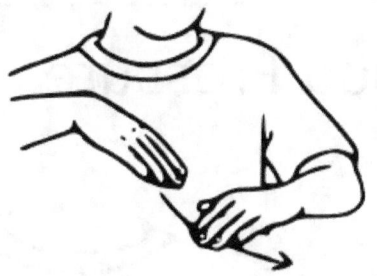	Ambulance 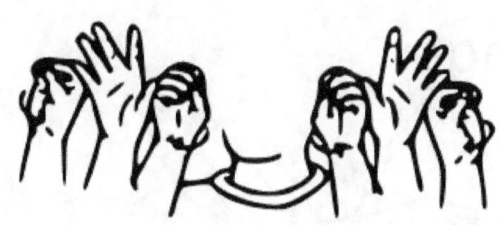
Emergency 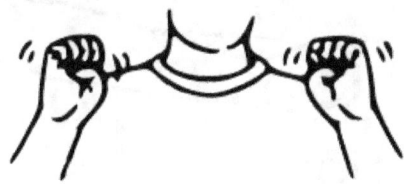	Hemorrage/Bleed 
Hospital 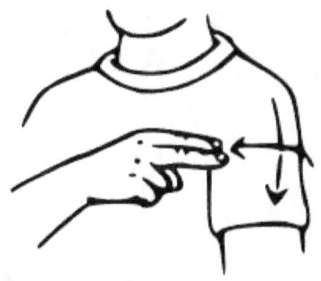	Discharge 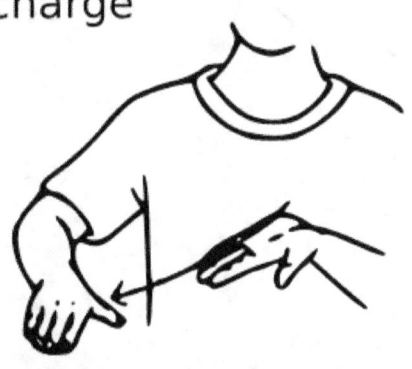

Medical Procedures

Bandage	Blood Pressure

Draw Blood	Injection
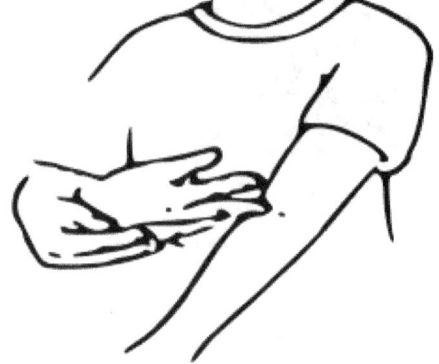	

Medical Procedures

Surgery

Stitch

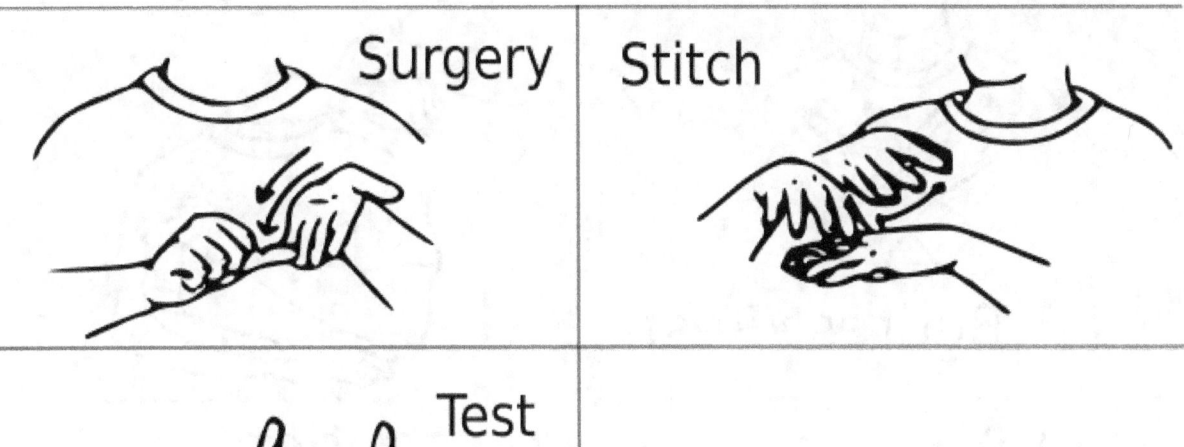

Test

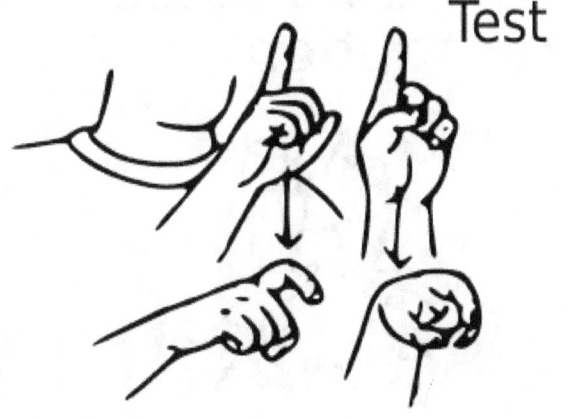

Remedies

Bedrest/Rest

Cast
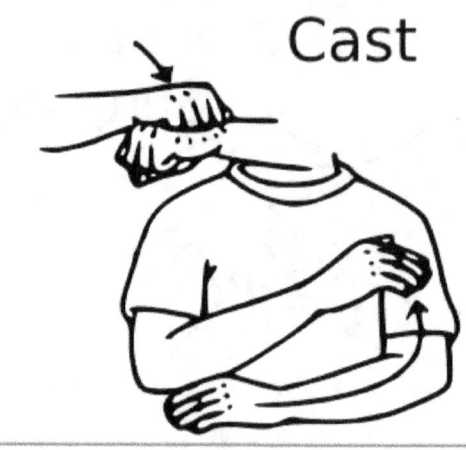

Crutches
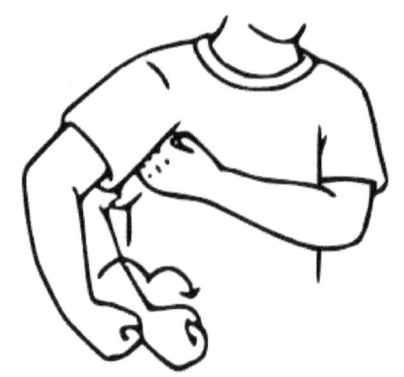

Prescription
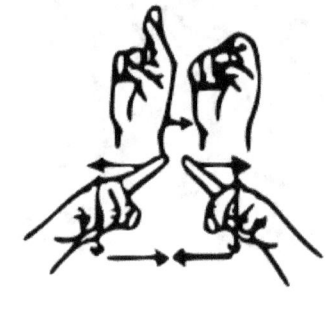

Wheelchair

Basic Words

Find your way out

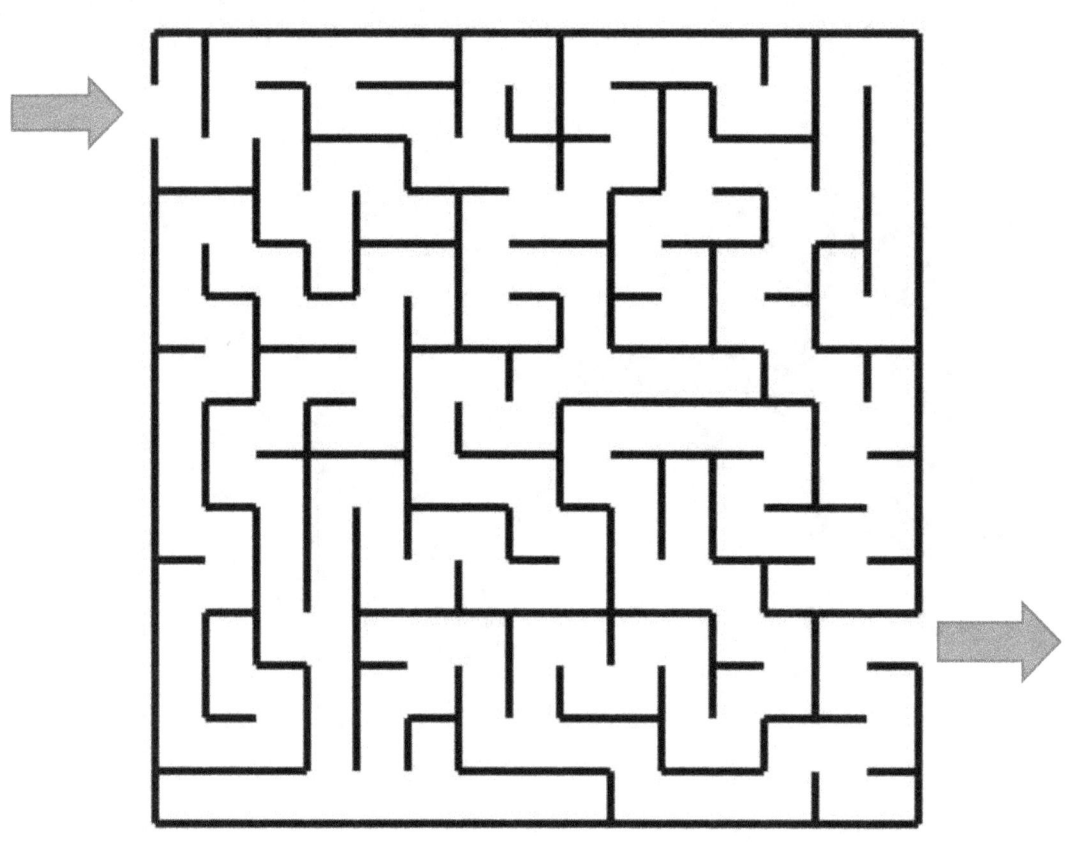

Find your way out

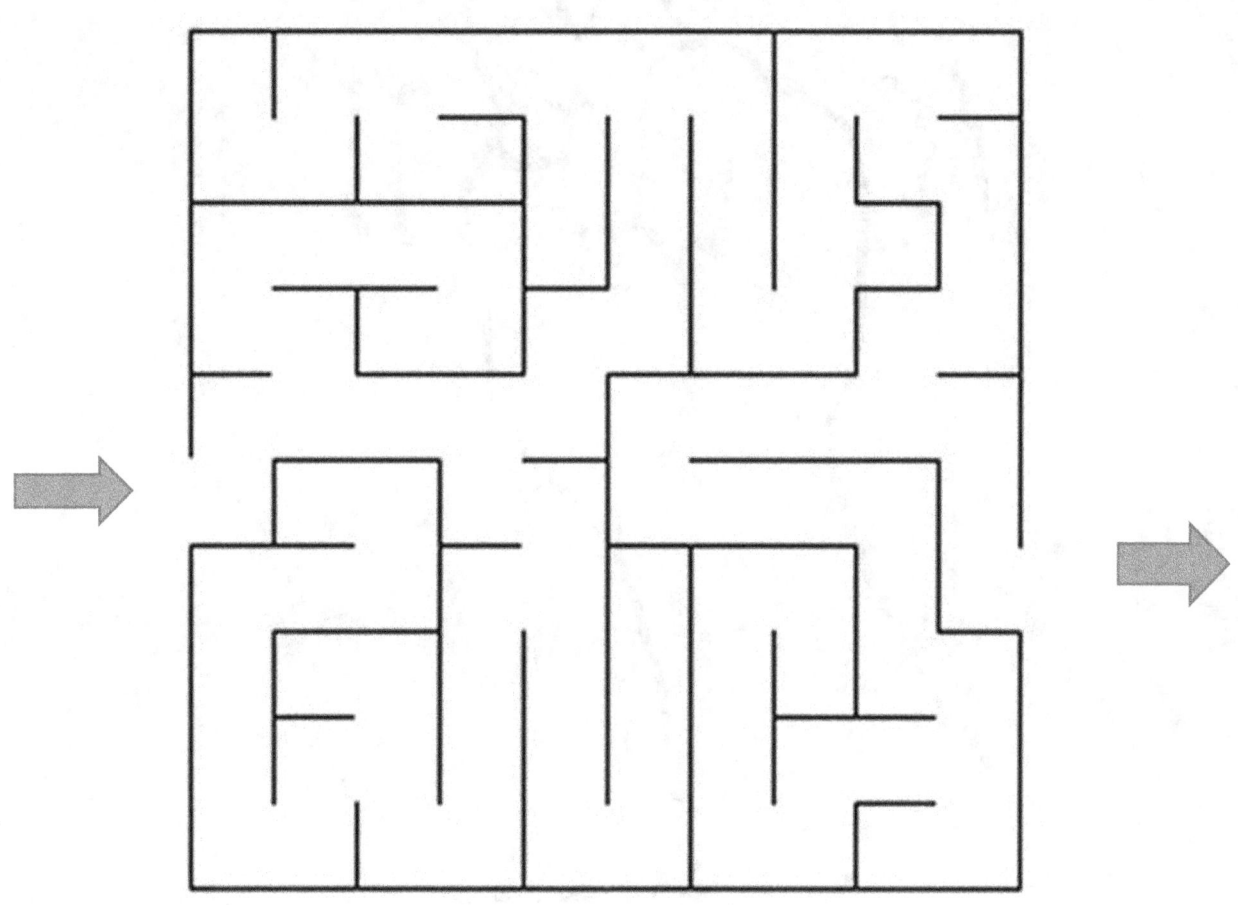

bathroom

book

goodbye

hello

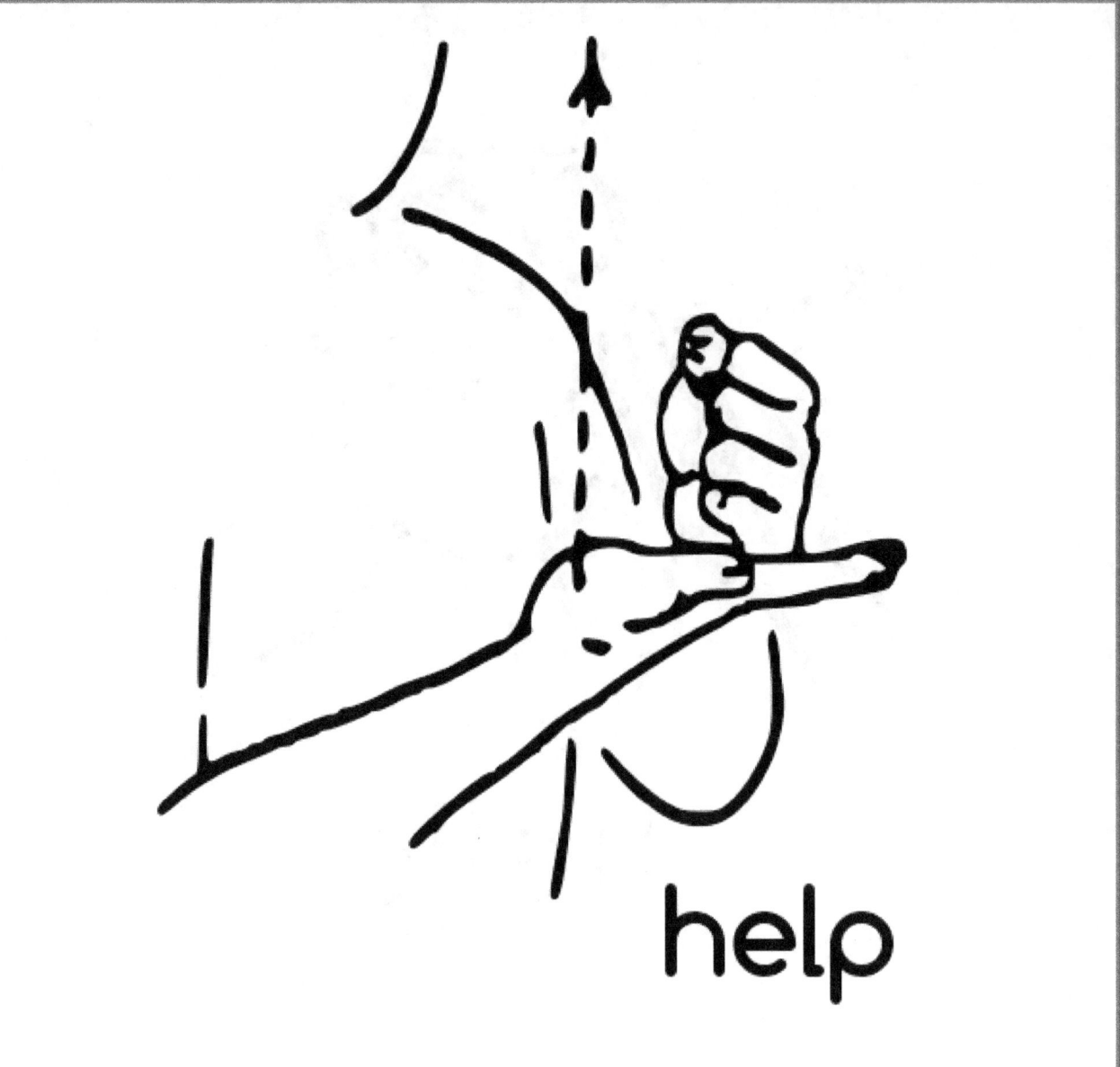

internet

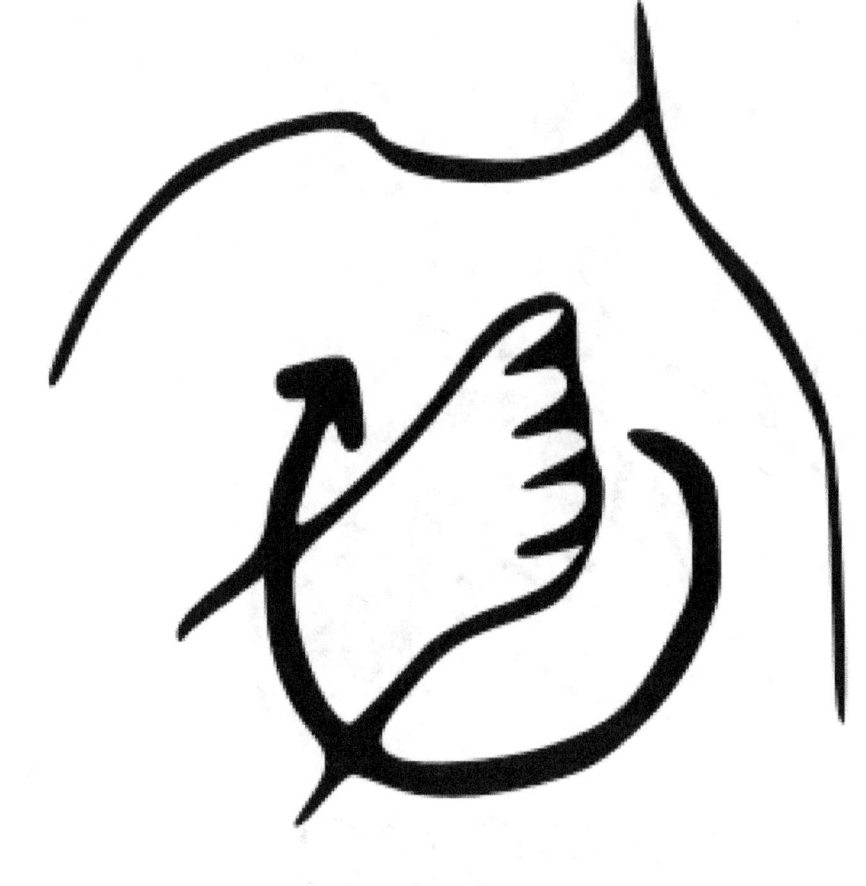

sorry

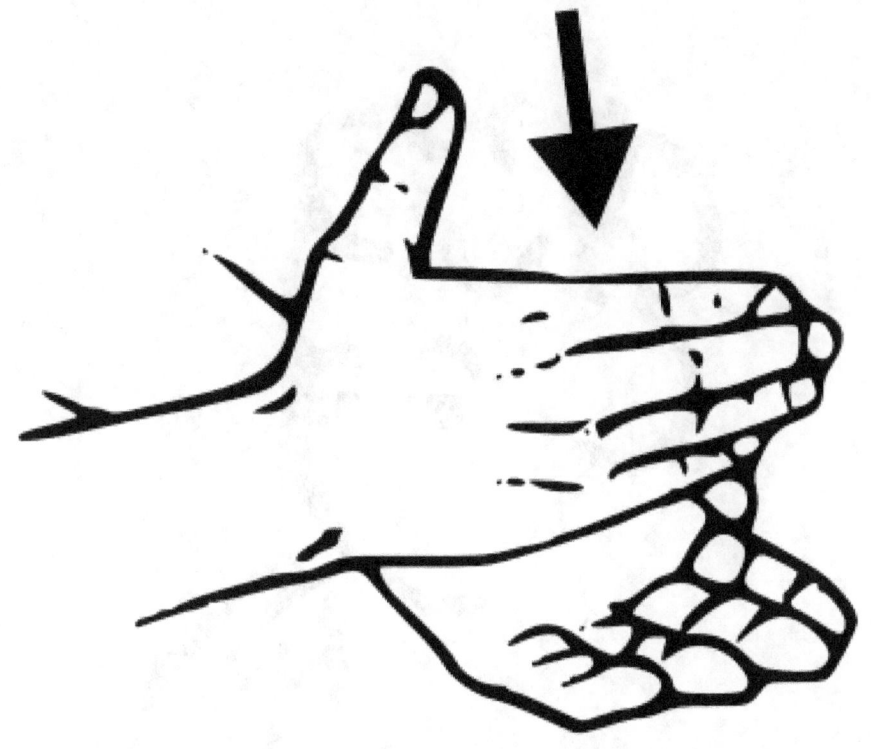

stop

thanks

thanks/good/welcome

what

when

where

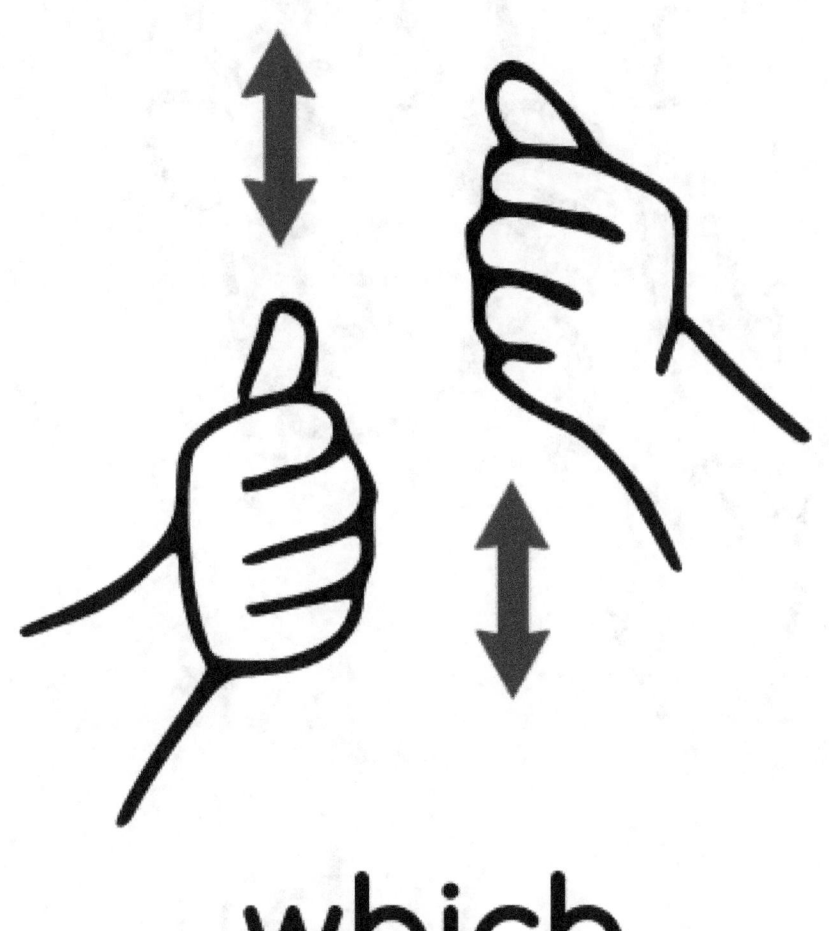

which

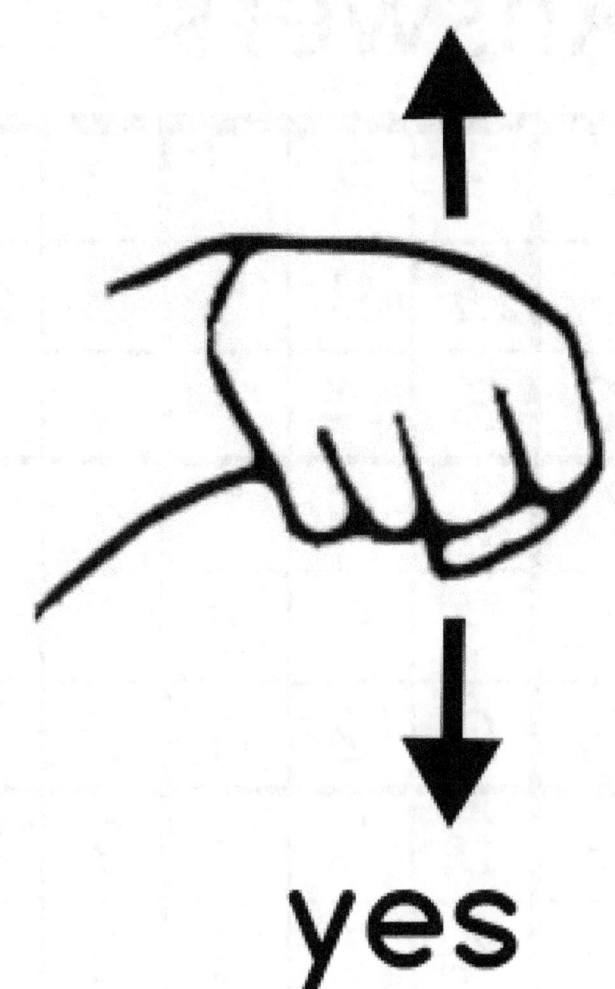

Answers

5	3	4	6	7	8	9	1	2
6	7	2	1	9	5	3	4	8
1	9	8	3	4	2	5	6	7
8	5	9	7	6	1	4	2	3
4	2	6	8	5	3	7	9	1
7	1	3	9	2	4	8	5	6
9	6	1	5	3	7	2	8	4
2	8	7	4	1	9	6	3	5
3	4	5	2	8	6	1	7	9

Disclaimer Statement

All information and content contained in this book are provided solely for general information and reference purposes. Smith Show Publishing LLC Limited makes no statement, representation, warranty or guarantee as to the accuracy, reliability or timeliness of the information and content contained in this Book.

Neither Smith Show Publishing Limited or the author of this book nor any of its related company accepts any responsibility or liability for any direct or indirect loss or damage (whether in tort, contract or otherwise) which may be suffered or occasioned by any person howsoever arising due to any inaccuracy, omission, misrepresentation or error in respect of any information and content provided by this book (including any third-party books.

BONUS SECTION
NAME THE ANIMAL HAND SECTION

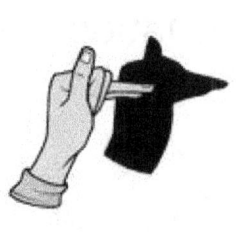   

 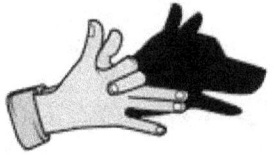  

BONUS SECTION
NAME THE ANIMAL

_ _ _ _ _ _ _ _ _ _

BONUS SECTION

NAME THE ANIMAL

__ __ __ __ __ __ __ __ __ __

BONUS SECTION

NAME THE ANIMAL

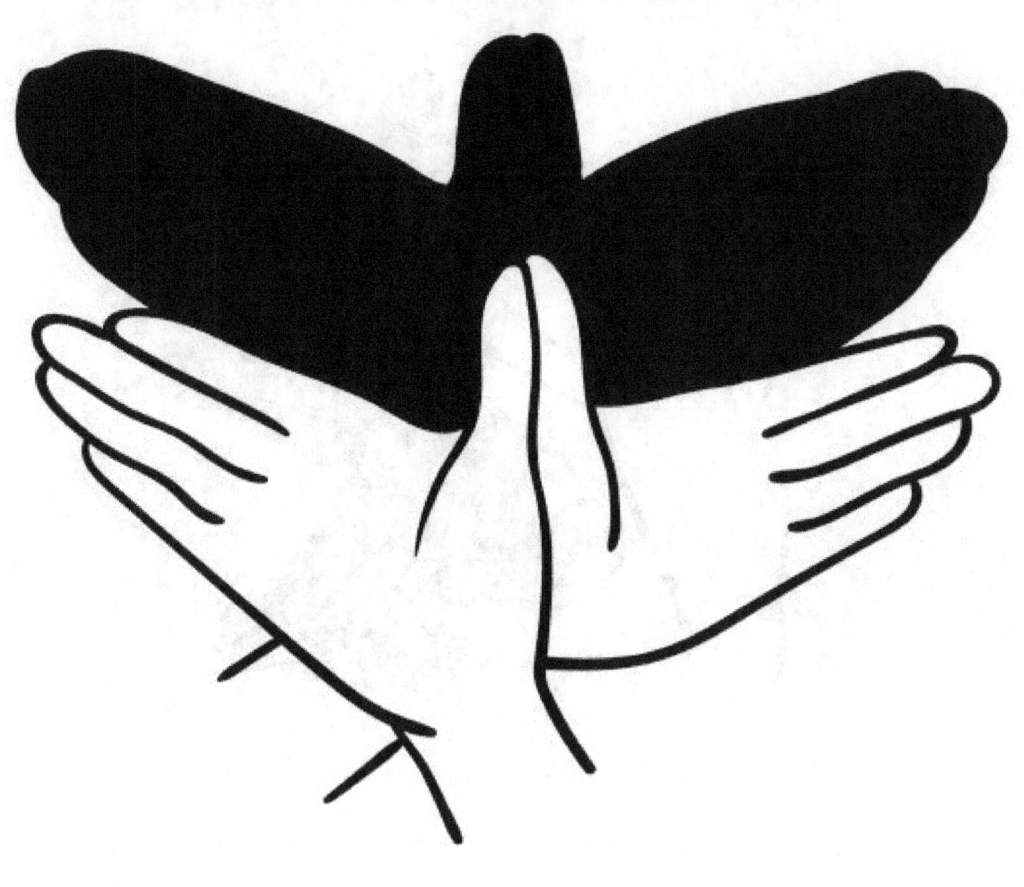

_ _ _ _ _ _ _ _ _

BONUS SECTION
NAME THE ANIMAL

BONUS SECTION

NAME THE ANIMAL

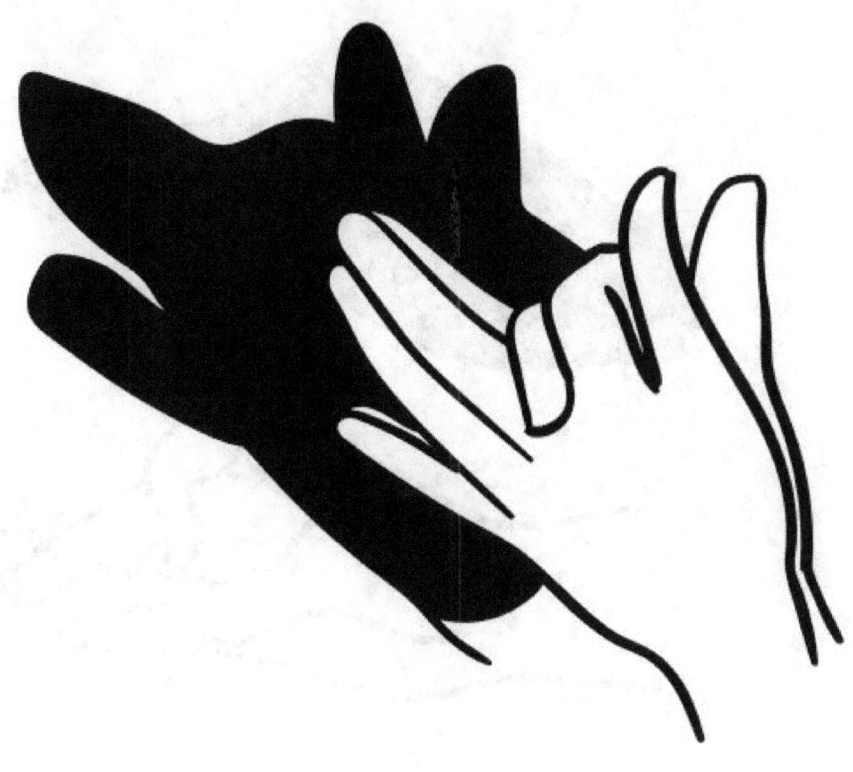

_ _ _ _ _ _ _ _ _ _

BONUS SECTION
NAME THE ANIMAL

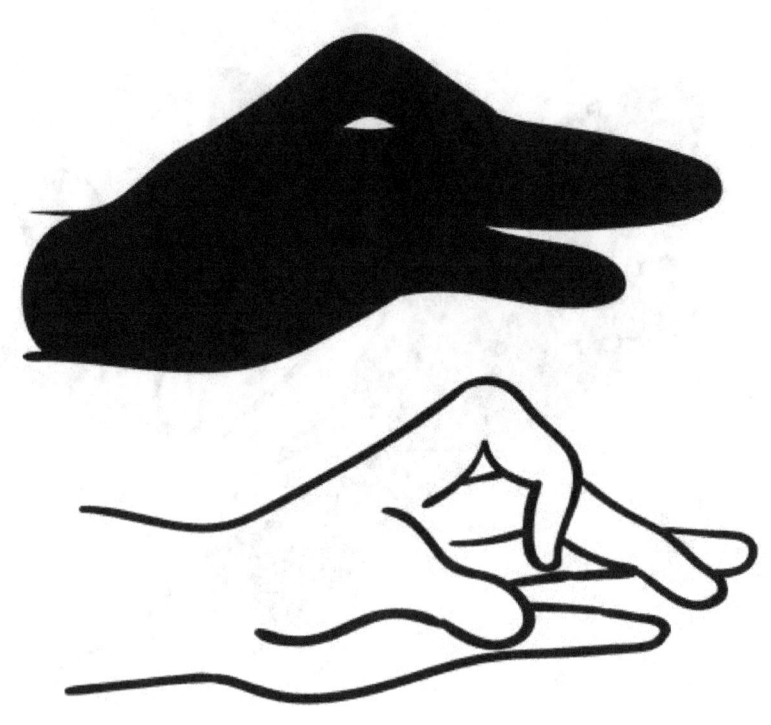

_ _ _ _ _ _ _ _ _

BONUS SECTION
NAME THE ANIMAL

_ _ _ _ _ _ _ _ _ _

BONUS SECTION

NAME THE ANIMAL

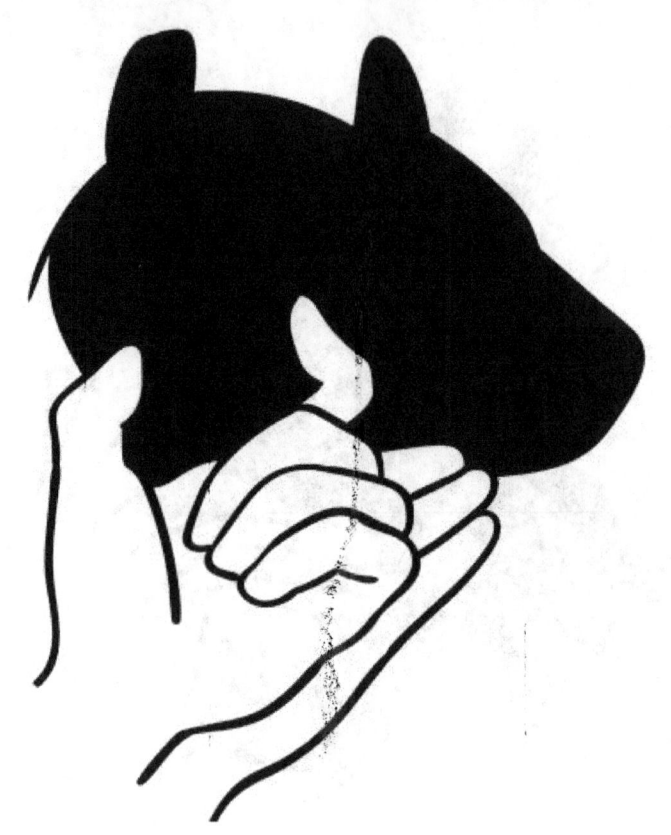

_ _ _ _ _ _ _

BONUS SECTION

NAME THE ANIMAL

_ _ _ _ _ _ _ _ _

BONUS SECTION
NAME THE ANIMAL

_ _ _ _ _ _ _ _ _ _

BONUS SECTION
NAME THE ANIMAL

_ _ _ _ _ _ _ _ _ _

BONUS SECTION
BODY SIGNS

Elbow Plank

Basic Plank

Elevated Side Plank

Elbow Plank (Knee)

Plank Leg Raise

Ball Plank

Bent Knee Side Plank

Plank Arm Reach

Ball Plank Reverse

Side Plank

Side Plank Knee Tuck (1)

Extended Plank

Side Plank Leg Lift

Side Plank Knee Tuck (2)

Reverse Plank

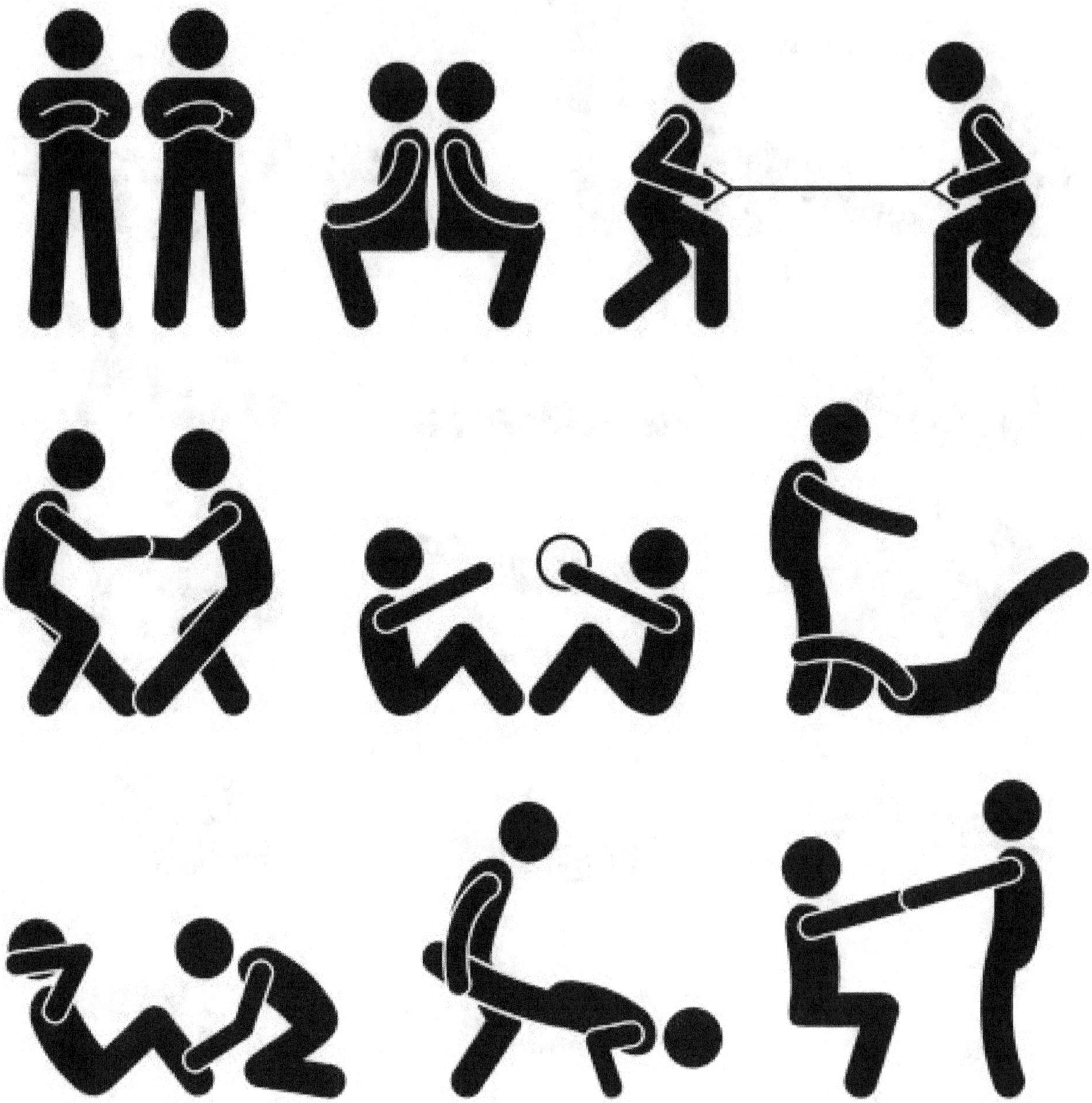

DRAW HAND SIGNS

DRAW HAND SIGNS

DRAW HAND SIGNS

DRAW HAND SIGNS

DRAW HAND SIGNS

DRAW HAND SIGNS

DRAW HAND SIGNS

DRAW HAND SIGNS

www.ingramcontent.com/pod-product-compliance
Lightning Source LLC
Chambersburg PA
CBHW081753100526
44592CB00015B/2419